What materials will choose to make up design?

GW00858461

Shops and Markets

All words in *italics* can be found in the glossary on page 31.
An index can be found on page 32.

Designed by Richard Crawford
Artwork by: Olivia Bown pp19, 25; Paul Daviz pp4 (top), 24;
Jenny Mumford p12; Sally Neave p4 (bottom), 5, 6, 17, 20;
Karen Tushingham p3.
Commissioned photography by Ollie Hatch

ISBN 0 00 317598 7

Published by Collins Educational London & Glasgow
A division of HarperCollins

First impression 1993.

Typeset by Dorchester Typesetting Group Ltd
Printed and bound in Hong Kong

The publishers would like to thank the following schools for their help:
Burghclere Primary School, Burghclere. Durley C.E. Primary School, Durley.
East Woodhay C.E. Primary School, East Woodhay. Grayshott Primary School, Grayshott.
Kimpton C.E. Primary School, Kimpton. King's Somborne C.E. Primary School, King's Somborne.
Otterbourne C.E. Primary School, Otterbourne. St. Bede's C.E. School, Winchester,
St. Joseph's R.C. Primary School, Aldershot. Weeke Primary School, Winchester.

The publishers would like to thank the following for permission
to reproduce photographic material:
The Body Shop pp22 (top), 23; Nicola Cornish p24;
Ducal Limited pp16, 17, 18 (top).

Shop style

Shopkeepers spend time thinking about how to attract customers. One way is to have an eye-catching shop front.

Flower shop

Food shop

Sports shop

Look at your local shops.

⭐ Which shop fronts make you want to go inside and buy the goods?

⭐ Which shop fronts do not make you want to go inside?

Make a class survey of your favourite and least favourite shop fronts.

Shop fronts and electricity

Problem

Work in a small team and design and make a shop front. Make sure the front is attractive to customers. All shops have electrics so you will need to add some lights, bells or alarms to your shop.

⭐ How will you switch your electrics on and off automatically?

You may need

card, wood, plastic, metal, lolly sticks, crayons, pens, a computer, a glue stick, tools, a ruler, bulbs, buzzers, wire, switches or computer control equipment

Find out how these switches work. 'Great Inventors' tells you about switches.

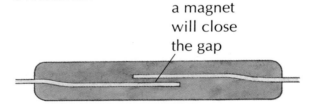

a magnet will close the gap

A reed switch

A toggle switch

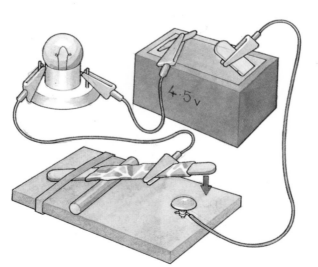

A press-to-make switch

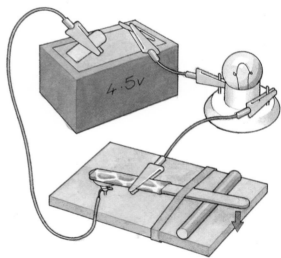

A press-to-break switch

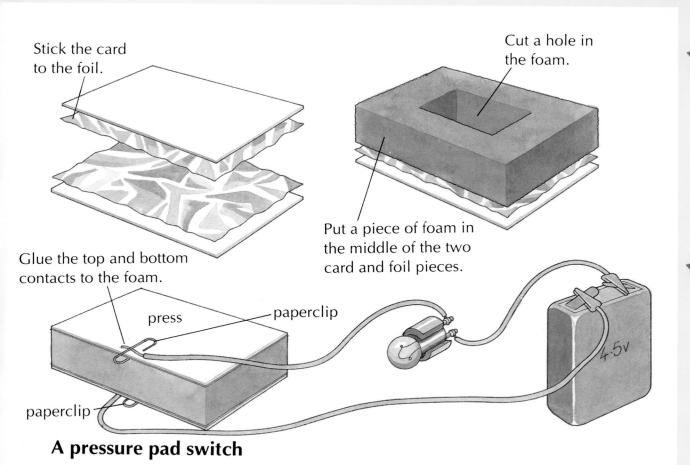

Stick the card to the foil.

Cut a hole in the foam.

Put a piece of foam in the middle of the two card and foil pieces.

Glue the top and bottom contacts to the foam.

press

paperclip

paperclip

4.5v

A pressure pad switch

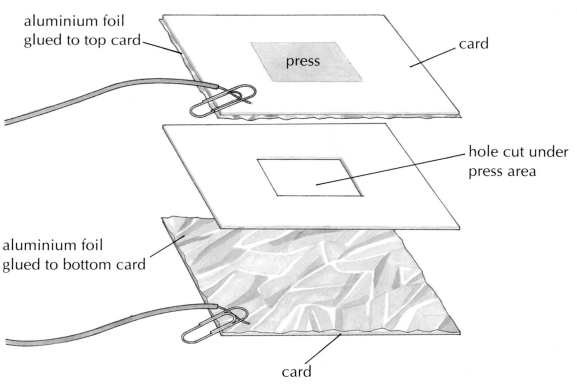

aluminium foil glued to top card

press

card

hole cut under press area

aluminium foil glued to bottom card

card

A membrane switch

Which is best for your purpose?

Shop structures

The shop front is a *structure*. All structures must support themselves as well as the things that are built on to them.

You can:

◆ Score and fold card or correx to make it stand up.
◆ Use wood to make a stronger structure.
◆ Use triangles for strength.

Look at *frame structures*. Look at *shell structures*.
Which would be best for your purpose?

Remember to do these skills neatly.

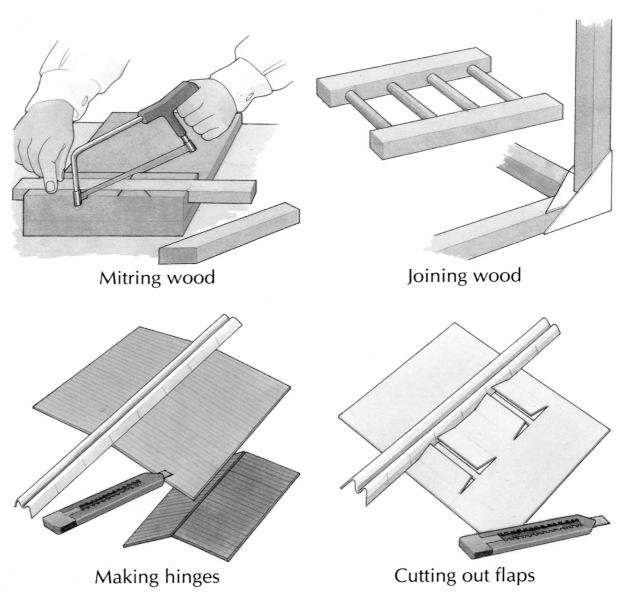

Mitring wood

Joining wood

Making hinges

Cutting out flaps

Designing your shop front

Find your purpose.

⭐ What do you want your shop front to do?
⭐ What might your customers like?
⭐ How can you find out?

Try out ideas.

Make a prototype. Improve your ideas. Do not forget the electrics!
'Great Inventors' will help you to find out more about electricity.

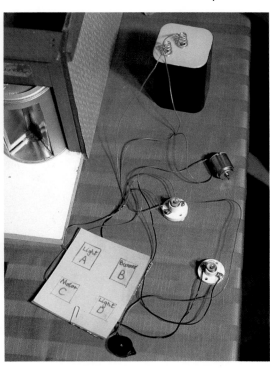

▲ This team is making a pressure pad which will make a light work in their shop.

▶ Another team made a membrane switch for the electrics in their shop.

How will you make your shop front look attractive:
Colour? Careful lettering? Materials?

... and making the shop front

Make your final design. Show what you will make and the materials you will use.

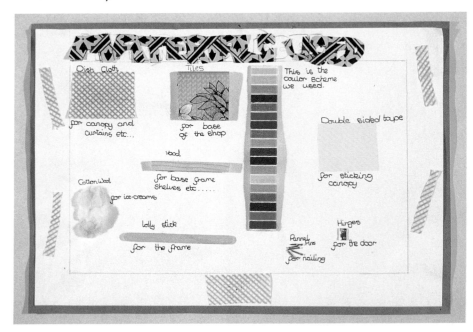

Organise yourselves!

- ✪ How will you work?
- ✪ How will you divide the jobs in your team?
- ✪ Is your work area ready?
- ✪ Are your materials ready?

Go! Make your shop front.

- ✪ Are you making everything well?
- ✪ Are you improving anything?

An ice-cream shop.

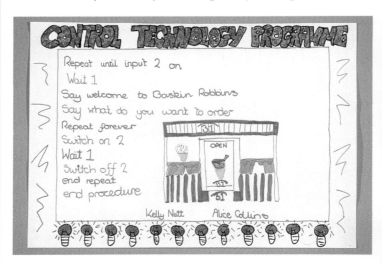

Testing

How will you test your shop front to see if it fits its purpose?

▲ Testing the pressure pad switch for the light.

How do other teams' shop fronts fit their purpose?

9

Other children's ideas

Do you think these shops fit their purpose?

▲ The designers of this shop made some cakes to sell in their shop.

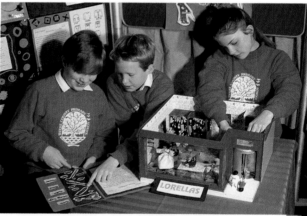

▲ How do you think the door works on this shop?

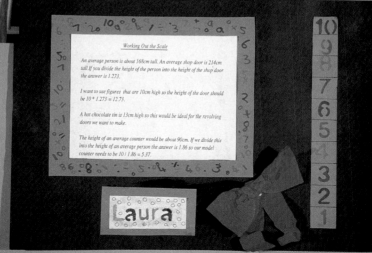

Finding a market

The price of goods is important. They must not be too expensive so people will not buy them. They must not be too cheap so the shopkeeper does not make any profit.

◆ The appearance of goods is important.
They must be well made and look good.
◆ The goods must do what they are intended to do.
They must work and not wear out immediately.
◆ Goods must be designed and made for a particular *market*.
Some goods are only suitable for children.
Some goods are only suitable for adults.

Problem
Design and make something to sell in your school shop. It must be something which children would like to buy.

✪ What might be needed?
✪ Will you make something new or improve a product?
✪ What will you charge?
✪ How much will children be prepared to pay?
✪ How much will the materials cost?
✪ Will you need to add on other costs?
✪ How will you use the Inventor's Roundabout?

Activity 9 is one idea you could follow, or you may wish to find your own opportunity.

Party masks

Imagine that party masks are an important new fashion craze. Just about everyone wants to wear them. Everyone wants to go to a party in disguise!

Problem

Work in a team of four. Design and make a party mask to sell in your school shop. Other teams in your class could work on the same problem.

You may need

> card, sequins, fabric scraps, glitter, paper for decorating, pens, elastic, scissors

Important

◆ Before you begin make sure all the materials are priced.

◆ If you use more materials you will put the cost up.

What do people want? Find a market. Find out how much people will pay.

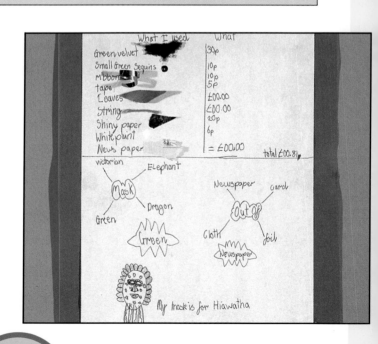

Designing the mask

✪ What is your purpose?

Brainstorm for ideas! Check that people really want your mask.
Try out some designs.

Make a prototype
You could bring a party mask into
school. Cover it with aluminium foil.
Wrap paper bandages round the front of
the mask leaving the back unbandaged.
When the bandaging is dry, unwrap the
foil and take out the shop-bought mask.

Now you can start thinking about the
decoration. Try out different colours.

Colours can be:

| fun | frightening | friendly | anything else? |

Try out different trimmings.
They can be:

- glamorous
- gorgeous
- anything else?
- glittery
- gory

Try out different textures.
Materials can be:

- smooth
- silky
- fluffy
- rough
- furry
- anything else?

13

Pricing your mask

Make a final design. Show all the materials you intend to use on your mask.

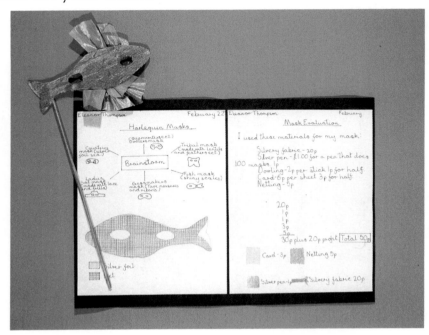

Make your mask. Remember to make your mask look good on the inside as well as on the outside.

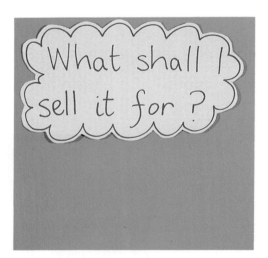

What shall I sell it for?

- ⭐ Can you sell your mask?
- ⭐ Is the price right?
- ⭐ Are the goods well made?
- ⭐ Which kind of mask is most popular?
- ⭐ What do people like most about it?

Testing your mask

You could make a lot of masks like real *manufacturers* do.

Or would your customers prefer something else?
What might they like?

Making furniture

These two pieces of furniture are designed and made by a famous furniture company. The furniture is made in their factory and then sold to shops. The type of furniture they make is called *reproduction furniture*. Discuss with your class what this means.

The company is now thinking about designing and making children's furniture. Can you help them? First find out more about furniture.

Collect

Furniture catalogues and dolls furniture.

✪ Which kind of furniture do you like?
✪ What kind of wood is the furniture made from?

Collect

Different woods that are used for furniture.

✪ How are they the same?   ✪ How are they different?
✪ Have they been *treated*?   ✪ Have they been painted?
✪ Have they been *stained*?

From forest to furniture

The furniture company uses Redwood pine trees which are grown in Sweden. Redwood pine has exactly the right sort of *grain* and small *knots*. It is also strong and looks attractive.

Redwood pine trees grow quickly and reach the right size for cutting after about 25 years.

After the pine tree has been cut down, the timber is shipped from Sweden to Britain and it is then taken by lorry to the company's factory in Andover, Hampshire to be made into furniture.

◆ On a map plot the journey of the Redwood trees from the forest to the factory.

◆ Look at the grain of pine wood. Look at the knots. Which wood do you think is best for furniture?

Wood is stronger if it is used this way. It is also harder to cut as you cut across the grain.

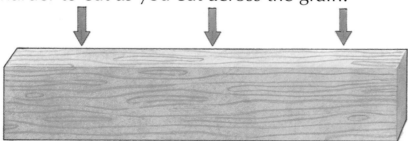

Wood is less strong if it is used this way.

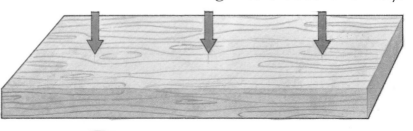

Quality furniture

The company's purpose is that their furniture must:

◆ look good   ◆ work well   ◆ last a long time.

Why do you think these things are important?
The way things are made makes a difference to fitness for purpose.
It makes a difference to the quality of the furniture.

Problem

Design and make a model of some furniture that will be suitable for the new children's range. You will need to work out what your furniture will cost.

First explore furniture.
Look at the structure.

⭐ What kind of structure does it have?
⭐ What parts make the structure strong?
⭐ What parts need to balance?
⭐ What lines of *symmetry* do different pieces of furniture have?

Try and make a chair, table or bed with rolled paper tubes. What are the problems with furniture making?

Look at the way furniture is joined. How many different ways are there of joining? Do not forget to look at drawers and doors.

▶ These children are checking how hinges are made for cupboard doors.

Designing furniture

You will need

wide and narrow wood, dowel, fabric, glue, card, wood stains, paint, tools

Who might like your furniture:
- babies?
- toddlers?
- young children?
- older children?
- teenagers?
- anyone else?

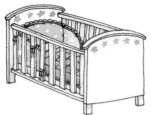

What style might be needed:
- nursery rhymes?
- Tudor?
- Victorian?
- other?

Do you want to make up a furniture questionnaire?

Do you want to look up any information?

Look at all the different designs there are for each kind of furniture that you can buy in the shops.

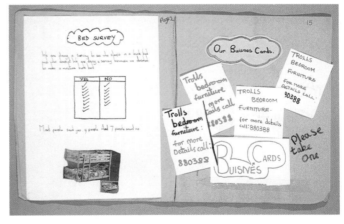

▲ A bed survey by Trolls Bedroom Furniture.

Design your furniture. How many designs can you make? Make your final design. Activity 17 gives you help on joining wood.

Shaping, finishing and joining wood

◆ Measure carefully.
◆ Cut carefully.

◆ Shape carefully.

◆ Finish beautifully.

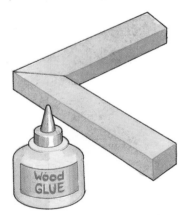

◆ Glue join.

◆ Dowel join.

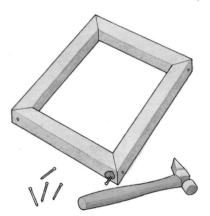

◆ Small panel pin join.

Other children's furniture

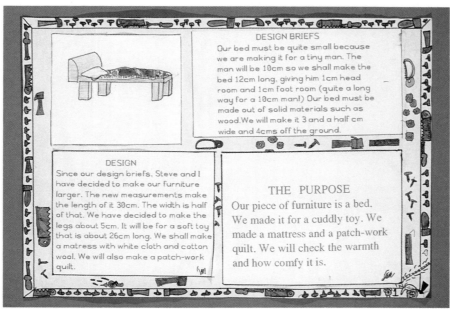

DESIGN BRIEFS
Our bed must be quite small because we are making it for a tiny man. The man will be 10cm so we shall make the bed 12cm long, giving him 1cm head room and 1cm foot room (quite a long way for a 10cm man!) Our bed must be made out of solid materials such as wood. We will make it 3 and a half cm wide and 4cms off the ground.

DESIGN
Since our design briefs, Steve and I have decided to make our furniture larger. The new measurements make the length of it 30cm. The width is half of that. We have decided to make the legs about 5cm. It will be for a soft toy that is about 26cm long. We shall make a matress with white cloth and cotton wool. We will also make a patch-work quilt.

THE PURPOSE
Our piece of furniture is a bed. We made it for a cuddly toy. We made a mattress and a patch-work quilt. We will check the warmth and how comfy it is.

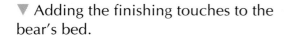

▶ Varnishing a chair for a cuddly toy.

▼ Adding the finishing touches to the bear's bed.

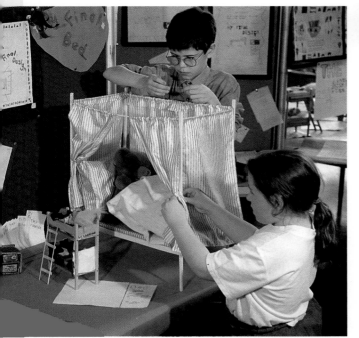

How will you cut, shape, join and finish your furniture? Does your furniture fit its purpose?

Our bodies

Have you noticed how many products help us to care for ourselves?

- ◆ Nail brushes
- ◆ Bubble baths
- ◆ Toothpaste and toothbrushes
- ◆ Shampoos
- ◆ Soaps

Make a class collection of things which keep you clean. Discuss with your class why each kind of product is needed.

Afterwards work in a small team and choose a product. Discuss whether the product and its package, if it has one, is a good design. Say whether the product fits its purpose.

Does it:

- ✪ Do what it is supposed to do?
- ✪ Does it look good, smell good, feel good?
- ✪ Is the price right?
- ✪ Could anything be improved?

Draw a product.
Say whether it fits its purpose.
Would you like to improve anything?

The Body Shop

The Body Shop sells things which help us look after our bodies. All their products have been checked for fitness for purpose. Each product has been designed with someone in mind.

Before a product is designed and made the designer asks, "Who will need it? What is the market?"
Look at these products. What kind of a person would like these?

Choose a product from your display for:

◆ Girls only   ◆ Boys only
◆ Teenagers only   ◆ Everyone.

✪ Why would each group like and need it?
✪ Why would other groups not like or need it?

Now choose another product and design an advertisement.

✪ What kind of customer do you want to attract?
✪ What is your market?

Soap problems

Have you ever lost your
soap in the bath?

Here are two products which might help with this problem.

Soap boats
Soap boats can be made in the shape of
different fruits. They can float around in
the bath and are made from moulded
plastic.

Soap baths
Soap baths can be put on a table or shelf near the bath. They are
made from clay and then fired in a kiln. Afterwards the clay is glazed.

Problem
Design and make something to keep the soap safe while you are
in the bath.

Will your product be:

◆ Fun?   ◆ Fancy?   ◆ Plain?   ◆ Glamorous?

✪ Who would like it?   ✪ Who might need it?
✪ What problem will it solve?

Will your market be:

◆ Young children?   ◆ Older children?   ◆ Teenagers?
◆ Boys?   ◆ Girls?   ◆ Other people?

Fitness for purpose

Look at products which solve the soap problem.

⚙ What kind of structures are they?

⚙ What kind of shapes are they?

⚙ What are they made from?

⚙ How is the product joined?

⚙ How much might each one cost?

⚙ Do they fit their purpose? Try them out!

Brainstorm different ideas which could meet your purpose. What kind of materials could you use? Do you want to use plastic? Look at what there is to choose from. Think how you can help the environment by recycling plastics.

You could use see-through bottles in different colours. Bottles come in all shapes and sizes. They can be made from:

◆ Thick plastic
◆ Stiff plastic
◆ Easy-to-bend plastic.

Could you cut it? Could you change it? Could you stick it?

Designing

Do you want to use another material?
Correx? Clay? Wood? Metal? Paper bandaging?

This girl is cutting petals out of correx.

How can you make everything waterproof?
Look back at your ideas. Which fit your purpose?
Make your design. Use the tools carefully.

If you use plastic bottles:

◆ Saw first to make a small cut.
◆ Cut out the rest with scissors.

Use a cool glue gun to stick plastic. Remember to wear goggles.

Be careful

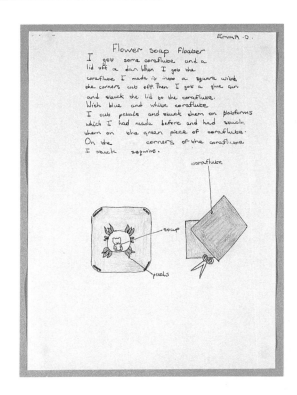

Add other materials to decorate your soap container. Remember it must look good. It must be good enough to sell. Keep thinking about your purpose and keep testing as you make it.

Other children's solutions

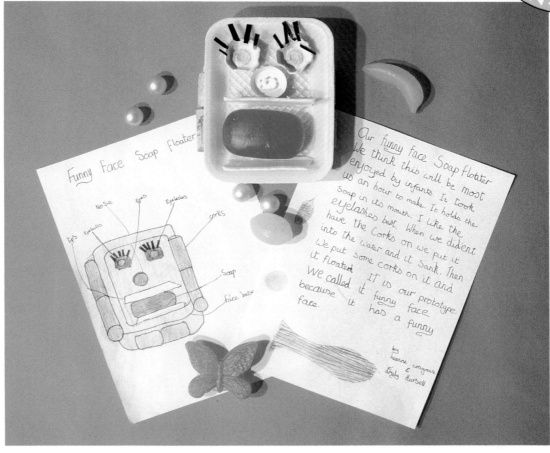

Funny Face Soap floater

Labels on the drawing: Nose, Eyes, Eyelashes, corks, lips, Eyebrows, Soap, face base

Our funny face Soap floater. We think this will be most enjoyed by infants. It took us an hour to make. It holds the soap in its mouth. I like the eyelashes best. When we didnt have the Corks on we put it into the water and it Sank. Then we put some corks on it and it floated. It is our prototype. We called it funny face because it has a funny face.

by Leanne Cosgrove & Emily Hutsell

▲ A prototype soap floater.

⭐ What tests will you make?

A belt bag

A belt bag can hold important things and keep them safe when you are moving around.

Look at the bags in the picture.

✪ Do you think they fit their purpose?
✪ Are there any problems with the design?
✪ How could you improve the belt bag?
✪ Do you think a different solution is needed?

Look at each part of the belt bag:

◆ the structure
◆ the shape
◆ the fastenings.

✪ How is it joined?

Draw the bag and put in each part. Say whether each part fits its purpose. What improvements can you suggest to each part?

Design for a purpose

Shops always need to have new products to sell.
Shops always need improved products.

Problem

Design your own belt bag. Make careful drawings. Make a paper pattern. Think about how you could make your bag.

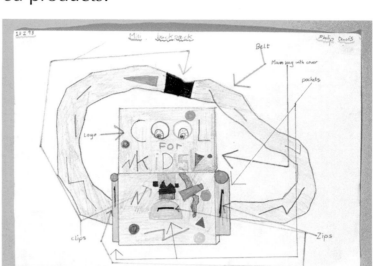

✪ Are you going to sew your bag?
   Will you use:
   ◆ blanket stitch?
   ◆ running stitch?
   ◆ back stitch?
   ◆ machine stitch?

✪ How are you fastening your bag? Will you use:
   ◆ zips?   ◆ press studs?   ◆ buttons?
   ◆ buckles? ◆ Velcro?

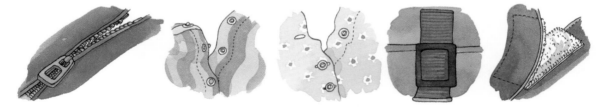

Make your final design.
What materials will you use?
Plan how you will make your bag.

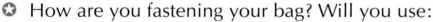

Designing our Security (Bum) Bag.

We chose felt for the material because it was easy to sew and it had a nice feeling to it. Black was the colour we used because it is a good back ground colour. We chose a gold black and red colour scheme. We based it on the flower that we chose first.

To fasten it we used velcro as a shutter and D-rings to hold the belt together. To join the sides together we did blanket stiching, it lookes very effective when it is finished.

We can change the structure by taking out the cardboard sides and change it from a ridged bag to a soft one. You can also take the belt off.

All in all we think that we have made a good job of it.

The people in the team are:
   Sara Young
   Charlotte Anisworth
   Carly Willard

Quality products

What is your purpose?
Have you drawn a final design?

Make your bag.
Test your bag.

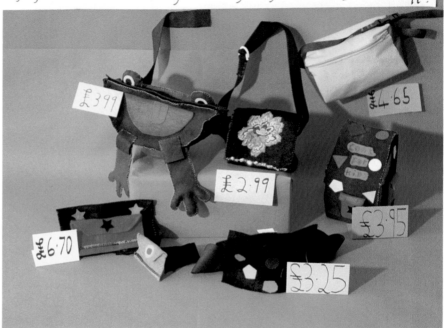

Does your product fit its purpose?

Make up your design. Make it as appealing as you can.

If you were to make your design again, would you change it?

£3.99

£4.65

£2.99

£3.95

£6.70

£3.25

Glossary

frame structure A structure that has its support on the inside.

grain   The way fibres lie to make patterns in wood.

knot   A dark, hard, round spot in wood which shows where a branch once grew.

manufacturer Someone who makes something to sell.

market   The demand for certain types of goods.

reproduction furniture Furniture made today to a style made years ago.

shell structure A structure that has its support on the outside.

stain   To change the colour of wood.

structure The way something is organised. It refers to the shape and the way different parts connect.

symmetry A feature or pattern that is repeated on the other half of an object.

treat   To cover wood with a special liquid that preserves or protects it.

Index